On the Story Mat

Barnabas

Best friends

by Brian Ogden

Bible stories for young readers

Acknowledgment

Mrs Gill Grainger, Deputy Head Teacher at Roebuck Infant School in Stevenage, has made an invaluable contribution to this series by reading all the manuscripts and using the stories with her children.

We are most grateful to Gill and to all the children at Roebuck Infant School for their help and encouragement.

Published by
The Bible Reading Fellowship
Peter's Way, Sandy Lane West
Oxford OX4 5HG
ISBN 0 7459 3566 4

First edition 1998

10 9 8 7 6 5 4 3 2 1

A catalogue record for this book is available from the British Library.

Printed and bound in Great Britain by Caledonian International Book Manufacturing Ltd.

Introduction

This is the second in a series of books for younger children. The setting is a reception class at Daisy Hill County Primary School. As with any classroom for younger children the story mat is an important feature. The teacher, Mrs Jolley, relates the happenings in the classroom to stories from the Bible. It is hoped that teachers and parents will be able to choose stories which relate to their immediate circumstances and that the children will soon become friends with Mrs Jolley's children.

In each book there are seven stories, three from the Old Testament and four from the New. Bible references are given to enable the context of the story to be enlarged on if required. Prayers relating to each story are included for use in an assembly or with a story at bedtime. These are both to be found at the end of each book.

So please come now and meet Mrs Jolley, together with David, Emma, James, Sarah, Joshua and his twin sister Rosie, Michael, Hannah, Nathan and last, but not least, Sam. As it says on the classroom door...

Welcome to Mrs Jolley's Class

Contents

Best friends

David and Joshua were sitting in the playhouse.

They were looking at a picture book together.

'You're my best friend,' said David.

'And you're my best friend too,' said Joshua.

Mrs Jolley heard the boys talking and smiled.

Emma and Hannah were working in the sand tray.

'Will you be my best friend?' asked Emma.

'Yes, please,' said Hannah, 'and you're my best friend.'

Mrs Jolley heard what the girls said to each other and smiled.

A little later Mrs Jolley spoke to all the children.

‘It’s time for our story.

Come and sit on the story mat, please.’

David sat next to Joshua
and Emma sat next to Hannah.

‘I’m going to tell you a story
about friends.

Friends are very special people.

Friends sometimes do very special
things for us.

One day Jesus was in a house.

Jesus was talking to a big crowd of people.

There were people everywhere.

There were people sitting on the chairs.

There were people sitting on the floor.

There were people looking in through the doors.

There were people listening through the windows.

Outside the house were five men.

One of the men was very ill.

The man who was ill lay on a mattress.

"What are we going to do?"
asked one man.

"I don't know," said the second man.

"We'll never get the mattress in there,"
said a third man.

"But we must," said the fourth man.

"Only Jesus can make him better."

“I’ve got an idea,” said the first one.

He whispered his idea to the others.

Two of the men climbed up the steps
to the roof of the house.

The two men took some tiles
off the roof.

Soon there was a big hole in the roof.

The men could see Jesus
through the hole.

The men tied a rope to the mattress
and lifted it on to the roof.

Very carefully they lowered their friend
through the hole.

The man on the mattress wondered what was happening.

Soon he was lying on the floor in front of Jesus.

Jesus spoke to the man who was ill.

"Get up," he said, "pick up your mattress, and go home."

The man saw the love in Jesus' eyes.

He did what Jesus told him.

Jesus had made the man well again.

Outside the house he said a very big thank you to his friends,' said Mrs Jolley.

'That's what best friends would do,' said David.

I want my mum

It was Monday morning in Mrs Jolley's reception class.

And it was a very noisy
Monday morning.

Most of the children were
looking at books.

David, Joshua and Sarah had some big picture books.

Emma, Hannah and Michael were playing a word game.

They were all working quietly
and happily.

The noise was coming from Sam.

Sam was not happy.

Sam was crying and Sam was shouting.

Mrs Jolley put her arm round Sam.

Mrs Jolley tried to stop Sam from crying and shouting.

'I want my mummy!' shouted Sam.

'I want to go home!' shouted Sam.

The tears rolled down Sam's face on to Mrs Jolley's arm.

Mrs Jolley wiped Sam's tears with a tissue.

After a long time Sam stopped crying and shouting.

Sam just sat and sniffed.

'Time for a story, everyone,'
said Mrs Jolley.

The children came and
sat on the story mat.

Sam sat next to David.
David put his arm round Sam.

'Sometimes we miss our mummies
when we start school,' said Mrs Jolley.

‘I’m going to tell you a story about a boy called Samuel.

Samuel’s mummy was called Hannah and his father’s name was Elkanah.

For a long time Hannah couldn’t have any children.

Hannah went to God’s house and prayed.

She prayed that God would let her have a baby.

God heard her prayers and baby Samuel was born.

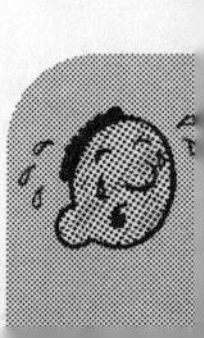

Hannah and Elkanah were very happy and thanked God for their baby.

One day, Hannah took Samuel to God's house.

Hannah spoke to the priest at God's house.

The priest's name was Eli.

"God gave me Samuel," said Hannah.

"I promised God that I would bring Samuel to you when he was old enough."

Samuel stayed with Eli and helped Eli to look after God's house.

Every year Hannah came
to visit Samuel.

Hannah brought him new clothes each time she came.

Hannah and Elkanah had
more children.

Samuel grew up to be very special,' said Mrs Jolley.

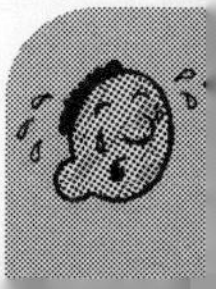

‘He must have been very brave,’
said David, ‘to leave his mummy.’

‘He was, and so is our Sam,’
said Mrs Jolley.

And David and Sam went off to play.

Presents

It was the first day back at school after the Christmas holidays.

The children were talking about their Christmas presents.

'I had the Man United football strip,' said Michael.

'I got a pram for my best doll,' said Sarah.

'I had a watch,' said Joshua.

'And I've got a...'

'Children,' said Mrs Jolley,
'please come and sit down.'

The children stopped talking and
sat down on the story mat.

'I wonder if anyone can guess what I
had for Christmas?' asked Mrs Jolley.

'If you look hard you might
be able to see it.'

All the children stared at Mrs Jolley.

Emma put up her hand.

'I think you've got a new necklace,' she said.

'Well done,' said Mrs Jolley. 'Emma is right.

My husband gave me a lovely gold chain.'

And Mrs Jolley lifted the chain and showed the children how it shone.

'My gold chain reminded me of some special presents.

Do you remember before Christmas we thought about Jesus being born?

When he was a little bit older he had some rather unusual visitors.

They had come a very long way to see Jesus.

These men were very clever.

They were so clever they used to tell their king what he should do.

We usually call them the
three wise men.

When they found Jesus they each
gave him a present.

The first wise man gave him
some gold.

Gold is the most precious metal and
it used to be given to kings.

The second wise man gave Jesus some perfume called frankincense.

Frankincense is used in some churches to make a nice smell.

The third wise man gave Jesus some myrrh.

Myrrh is a special ointment used when somebody in a hot country dies.

These were rather strange presents for baby Jesus.

But, you see, Jesus is a king and
so he was given gold.

Jesus is God's son whom we worship.

And Jesus died on the special day
we call Good Friday.

So perhaps they were the right
Christmas presents for Jesus,'
said Mrs Jolley.

'Now, it's time you told me about
your best present.'

My little brother

Rosie and Hannah were working in the water tray.

They wore their plastic aprons to keep dry.

Rosie was watching a little yellow duckling bobbing up and down on the water.

Hannah had some small cups.

She was pouring water from one cup into another.

'My mummy's got an apron like
this one,' said Rosie.

'She wears it when she gives
my brother a bath.'

'Wish I'd got a brother,' said Hannah.

'It's nice having a baby brother,'
said Rosie.

'But he doesn't do anything,
he just eats and sleeps and cries!'

Mrs Jolley heard Rosie and Hannah talking.

It was nearly time for the story.

'Tidy up, please,' said Mrs Jolley.

'And then come and sit on the story mat.'

The children sat on the floor near Mrs Jolley's story chair.

Rosie sat next to Hannah.

'I'm going to tell you a story about a baby brother and his big sister,' said Mrs Jolley.

Rosie and Hannah looked at each other and smiled.

'This story happened a long time ago,' said Mrs Jolley.

'People called the Hebrews lived in a country called Egypt.

There were a lot of Hebrews.

The Egyptian king thought there were too many Hebrews.

The king told his soldiers to kill all Hebrew boy babies.

Soon after this a Hebrew baby boy was born.

His mother wanted to keep him safe.

She made a basket out of reeds.

She put the baby in the basket.

She hid the basket in some tall grass by the side of the river.

The baby's big sister hid nearby to see what would happen.

A princess, the daughter of the Egyptian king, came to paddle in the river.

She heard the baby crying and saw the basket in the tall grass.

She took the baby out and gave it a cuddle.

The baby's sister went to the princess.

"Your majesty," she said,
"would you like me to find someone
to look after the baby?"

"Yes," said the princess,
"and I will pay you."

The little girl took the baby back home.

The baby was looked after by his
own mother after all.

The baby's name was Moses.

He grew up to be a great man,' said Mrs Jolley.

'Perhaps my baby brother will be important too,' said Rosie to Hannah, as they went out to play.

Names are special

Half the children in Mrs Jolley's class were painting.

There was old newspaper on the tables and big pieces of white paper.

There were some brushes in a pot.

On each table were some plastic water pots — the sort that can't spill.

Mrs Jolley had poured out some paint into the paint pots.

David was standing next to a new boy whose name was Nathan.

'Why haven't you got a proper name like me?' asked David.

Nathan didn't look happy.

'I mean, David and Michael and Sam are proper names — not Nathan!'

‘’Tis a proper name,’ shouted Nathan.

He put his brush in the water pot and flicked it at David.

The water didn’t reach David but it did drop on to his painting.

David looked at his picture.

The red paint was running into the blue paint.

'Nathan's messed up my painting,' shouted David.

Mrs Jolley came over to the boys.

'What is the matter?' she asked.

'Nathan put water on my picture,' said David crossly.

Mrs Jolley looked at Nathan.

'What happened, Nathan?' she asked.

'David said my name wasn't a proper name,' said Nathan.

'He said it wasn't like his silly name.'

Mrs Jolley told the two boys to put their painting away and get out their reading books.

Soon it was time for the story.

Mrs Jolley called everyone by name to come and sit down.

'Emma, Michael, Hannah, James, Rosie, Joshua, Sarah, Sam, Nathan, David...'

'Names,' said Mrs Jolley,
'are very special.

Your mum and dad chose your name very carefully.

All names mean something.

Sarah means princess.

Clare means bright.

Some people have more than one first name.

One of Jesus' best friends had two names.

When he was at home he was called Simon.

But Jesus called him Peter.

Peter means rock.

Jesus told Peter he must be strong and firm like a rock.

Although Peter wasn't always strong and firm, Jesus still loved him.

I think Peter was pleased that Jesus had called him Peter.

I think Peter was proud to have been given that name.

We should all be proud to have the names we have been given.

We should never think someone else's name is silly because it isn't like ours.

After play we'll see what everyone's name means,' said Mrs Jolley.

David and George

George was a bully.

George was in Year Two.

George was taller and stronger than any of the boys and girls in Mrs Jolley's class.

At playtime George kicked the ball away from the boys.

At playtime George took sweets from the girls.

The children were frightened of George.

'He's a bully,' said Emma.

'But what can we do?' said James.

'I know what we can do,' said David.

David told the other children about his plan.

The next day the children were playing with a ball.

George came over to them and grabbed the ball.

David went up to him.

'Give us our ball back, George,' he said.

George laughed.

'Are you going to make me?' he asked.

All the children from Mrs Jolley's class came up behind David.

They all stood looking at George.

George looked at them.

George gave the ball to David and ran off.

After play the children sat on
the story mat.

'It's not easy to be brave,'
said Mrs Jolley.

'Today I'm going to tell you a story
about a brave shepherd.

A shepherd has to keep his sheep
safe from wild animals.

David was a very brave shepherd.

One day David's father took him away from his sheep.

He gave David a big basket of food.

There were loaves of bread and big round cheeses.

"Take it to your brothers, please, David," said his father.

David's brothers were in the army fighting the enemy.

Just as David reached his brothers
he heard a very loud shout.

The shout came from the other
side of the valley.

"It's Goliath," said David's brothers,
and they turned and ran away.

David looked at Goliath.

He was nearly three metres high.

He carried a very long spear.

He was very frightening.

Goliath shouted again.

"Choose one of your men to fight me," he shouted.

David spoke to his brothers.

"I'll fight him," he said.

His brothers just laughed.

"Go home and look after the sheep," they told him.

"This isn't a job for boys."

But the king heard what
David had said.

“How can you fight him?”
asked King Saul. “You’re just a boy.”

“I’m a shepherd, your majesty,”
said David.

“God has saved me from
lions and bears.

He will save me from this giant.”

David went out with his sling and killed Goliath.

David was not afraid of bullies.

But if you see a bully in school you must tell me,' said Mrs Jolley.

Thanks

It was Emma's birthday on Tuesday.

She was five years old.

On Wednesday morning Emma took some of her birthday cake to school.

She gave the cake to Mrs Jolley.

'Thank you, Emma,' said Mrs Jolley.

'We'll all have a piece at milk time.'

The children were busy doing number work for the first part of the morning.

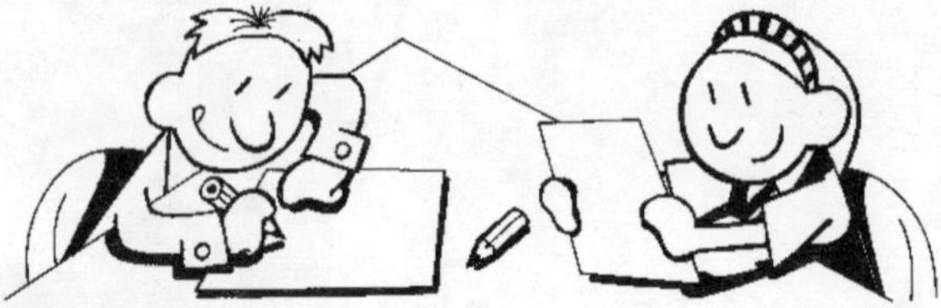

On David's table they were finding pairs of animals on their work sheets.

On Rosie's table they were guessing what weighed the most. Did two bananas weigh more than three potatoes? Then they used the balance to see if they were right.

Sarah's table were looking at pictures of a clock and writing down the time.

Mrs Jolley glanced at the classroom clock.

It was milk time. 'Today we've got a special treat.

Emma has brought us some of her birthday cake.

There's enough for everyone to have a small piece with your milk.'

The children took their cake from Emma. Mrs Jolley stood by listening.

After milk time the children sat on the story mat.

'One day Jesus was on a journey,' said Mrs Jolley.

'He was walking towards a village.

Coming out of the village were ten men.

They looked very unhappy.

They were unhappy because they all had a horrible disease.

Nobody had been able to make them better.

But they had heard that Jesus
made people well.

"Jesus, help us," they shouted.
"Make us well."

"Go and see the priests," said Jesus.

On their way to the priests they
all became well.

When one of the men saw he was well
he ran back to Jesus.

"Thank you, Jesus," he said.
"Thank you so much."

"There were ten of you," said Jesus.

"And only one has come back to say thank you."

When someone does something kind for us,' said Mrs Jolley, 'we should always say thank you.

I don't think many of you said thank you to Emma for her birthday cake.

Perhaps we could all do it now?'

Emma looked a bit shy when all the children said 'thank you' together.

'Now, please find your reading books,' said Mrs Jolley.

Bible references and prayers

The Bible references for each story are given to enable the background of the story to be used if required. By their nature the stories are short, make one point and omit much of the detail from the biblical passage. The stories can readily be the starting point for useful classroom discussion between the class teacher and the children. A prayer for each story theme is given. These prayers are based on the traditional approach of a response to the leader so that the children become involved in the prayers and make them their own.

Best friends

Luke 5:17–26

Lord God,
Thank you for our friends.
For the fun we have with our friends,
Thank you.
For all that we can share with our friends,
Thank you.
For the help our friends give us,
Thank you.
For all that they mean to us,
Thank you.

I want my mum

1 Samuel 1:1—2:10

Father God,
For mums and dads and
those who care for us,
Thank you.
For their love for us,
Thank you.
For all that they do for us,
Thank you.
For our homes and families,
Thank you.

Presents

Matthew 2:1–12

Dear Lord,
You have given us so much.
For the wonderful world we live in,
Thank you.
For all those who look after us,
Thank you.
For the love of our families and friends,
Thank you.
For Jesus, your present to us,
Thank you.

My little brother

Exodus 1:8—2:10

Father of all,
We pray for people who have special jobs.
For our Queen and the Royal Family,
Please be with them.
For our Prime Minister and government,
Please be with them.
For the leaders of all the countries in the world,
Please be with them.
For all who work for peace in your world,
Please be with them.

Names are special

John 1:35–42

Heavenly Father,
You love everybody.
When we have said nasty things,
We are sorry.
When we have done selfish things,
We are sorry.
When we have been unkind,
We are sorry.
When we are not nice to be with,
We are sorry.

David and George

1 Samuel 17:1–51

Loving Father,
There are people in your world
who are not happy.
For those who try to stop fighting,
Please be with them.
For those who take food to the hungry,
Please be with them.
For doctors and nurses
who make people well,
Please be with them.
For all who care for others,
Please be with them.

Thanks

Luke 17:11–19

Lord of all,
We thank you for our school.
For our teachers and
all who work there,
Thank you.
For our friends at school,
Thank you.
For all the fun we have at school,
Thank you.
For all the things we learn at school,
Thank you.